Frank Lloyd Wright's Taliesin West

Frank Lloyd Wright's Taliesin West

Photographs by Ezra Stoller

Introduction by Neil Levine

Princeton Architectural Press • New York

The BUILDING BLOCKS series presents the masterworks of modern architecture through the iconic images of acclaimed architectural photographer Ezra Stoller.

Contents

Frank Lloyd Wright at Taliesin West in 1951.

Introduction

Neil Levine

IN THE SPRING of 1946, when Ezra Stoller visited it for the first time,
Taliesin West had only recently been completed. The angular structures of the complex, built of volcanic stone and concrete, roofed with
canvas, were still completely isolated on 800 acres of unincorporated
land, in unspoiled desert, accessible only by a dirt road. Stoller was
commissioned to photograph Frank Lloyd Wright's headquarters in
Arizona, along with the earlier Taliesin in Wisconsin, by *Fortune* magazine for an article by George Nelson. This article gave many people
their first view, and certainly the first in color, of the vastly different
places in which Wright and his Taliesin Fellowship lived and worked.[1]
The following spring, Stoller's photographs were featured in the exhi-
bition *Taliesin and Taliesin West* curated by Philip Johnson at New
York's Museum of Modern Art. The publication and subsequent exhi-
bition made the obvious but by no means simple point that all of
Wright's architecture since the mid-1920s was conceived and produced

outside the urban environment in conditions as sophisticated as they were remote from the conventional world of professional practice.

Within the framework of modern architecture, Wright was unique in this regard. Le Corbusier had his office in the center of Paris and lived in an apartment house (of his own design) just outside the city limits, in an upscale, middle-class neighborhood. When Mies van der Rohe came to America to head the architecture school at the Illinois Institute of Technology (IIT), he worked in a downtown Chicago office not too far from the apartment he rented in a very *bürgerlich* neo-Renaissance building on the city's well-heeled Near North Side. Although Walter Gropius built himself a single-family house in the elegant Boston-Cambridge suburb of Lincoln, he did his teaching and design work in town. When an architect such as Rudolf Schindler or Alvar Aalto, not to speak of Paolo Soleri or Bruce Goff, seems to escape this pattern to a lesser or greater degree, it is more often than not attributable to some connection with or influence from Frank Lloyd Wright.

At the very beginning of his career, Wright decided that the commercial atmosphere of the city was not particularly favorable for the creation of architecture as a "fine art" and so, in 1898, he moved his practice to a studio added to the suburban Oak Park house he had designed for his family nine years earlier.[2] In this, as in much of what he did and thought at the time, he was following the example of the British Arts and Crafts movement. One might therefore think that when he left the metropolitan area of Chicago in 1911 to establish his home and office in the farming community of Hillside, in southcentral Wisconsin, he was still under the sway of C. R. Ashbee, who relocated the Guild of Handicraft from the East End of London to the Cotswold village of Chipping Campden in 1902. But Taliesin, as Wright called his new base of operations, was nothing like that predecessor, nor exactly like any other, be it Augustus Welby Pugin's

Taliesin, Hillside, Wisconsin, begun 1911. View looking northwest.

medieval monastery-like home and studio at Ramsgate (1843–47) or William Morris's neo-Gothic Red House at Bexley Heath (1859–60).

Taliesin had no such historical pretensions. It was designed to function as a modern country estate in the new automobile age, with all of the advantages that modern technology might afford. It would contain not only the architect's residence and office but housing for a growing staff of draftsmen and workers. A school, or at least a training program, may also have been envisaged from the beginning. All the various elements of the multipurpose program, which included self-subsistence farming, were disposed along the contours of a hill, just below its crown, in a continuous though rambling structure of local stone, plaster, and wood commanding views over the valley and the Wisconsin River. The name Taliesin, which in the Wright family's native Welsh means "shining brow," refers both to the appearance of the house on the hill slope and to the sixth-century poet-prophet celebrated throughout Welsh mythology and folklore.

Taliesin embodied Wright's vision of the unity of living and working. But more than merely a solution to the problem of shelter, it was a place where Wright could constantly—and obsessively—experiment with design, in three dimensions, with actual materials. It was, in effect, his sketchbook. As a direct and unadulterated expression of his most personal thoughts on architecture—his friend the sculptor Richard Bock called it a "self-portrait"—it also became a powerful form of self-promotion and advertising.[3] Prospective clients were invariably invited to Taliesin to get a taste of what a building by its master would be like.

Taliesin took on an additional role in 1932 when it became the home of the Taliesin Fellowship. The idea for the Fellowship can be traced back to 1928, when Wright and his third wife, the former Olgivanna Lazovich, conceived the idea of establishing an apprenticeship-based, communitarian-style "school of the allied arts" at the Hillside property. Significantly, it was in the same year that the two

Wright in his office at Taliesin in 1945.

first went to Arizona, apparently deciding that it would be a perfect place to spend the winter months. What brought Wright to Phoenix in January 1928 was an offer from Alfred Chase McArthur, a former employee at the Oak Park studio and son of a former client, to consult on the design of the luxury Arizona Biltmore Hotel that he and his two brothers were about to begin building. With no other work in sight, and being forced to vacate Taliesin temporarily for financially-incurred legal reasons, Wright jumped at the opportunity. Near the middle of their four-month stay, Wright received a commission of his own for a rival and even more exclusive resort hotel, this one to be built not within the city limits but on a remote desert site south of Phoenix, on the slopes of what were then called the Salt River Mountains (now the Phoenix South Mountains). The hotel was to be a branch of the Mission-style San Marcos Hotel in Chandler, a small town located a little over 10 miles to the east of the proposed site.

Design for the San Marcos-in-the-Desert Hotel began during that first stay in Phoenix and continued through December at Taliesin, to which the Wrights, now married, were finally allowed to return. The plan was always to go back to Arizona the next winter to complete work on the project *in situ*. Partly for economic reasons, though also to experience firsthand what living in the desert might be like, Wright decided to build a seasonal camp, which he called Ocatilla, just south of the hotel site, with living and working quarters for the fifteen people who made the trip from Wisconsin in January 1929. The canvas-topped wood cabins were joined together by a zigzagging board-and-batten wall. This enclosed an interior court formed by the ridge of a low mound along the slopes of which the units were disposed. The same 30/60-degree geometry that governed the plan of the hotel was used in the camp not only in plan but also in section to create the angular shape of the canvas roofs, themselves meant to reflect the profiles of the surrounding mountains.

Wright's intention was to return to Ocatilla for the winter season of 1930 to supervise construction of San Marcos-in-the-Desert, but, due to the stock market crash, the project was shelved. With the creation of the Fellowship and the expense and difficulty of keeping it functioning throughout the year in Wisconsin (the winter heating costs at Taliesin were astronomical), the idea of a permanent winter headquarters in Arizona began to take on a renewed sense of urgency. The entire group eventually made the trip in 1935 and again in 1936, both times staying at rented quarters in Chandler. Wright started looking for property on which to build and actually put down a deposit on land in the Santan Mountains, southeast of Chandler, in 1936, but the deal fell through. When he and Olgivanna returned alone to Arizona in the early spring of 1937, they looked closer to Phoenix and, in December, finally settled on land in Paradise Valley, about 26 miles northeast of the city, where they were soon joined by the entire Fellowship. Planning and construction began in January 1938.[4]

The site of Taliesin West lies high above the Salt-Gila River Valley and has a magnificent view over the entire region. It is closed in and protected to the north by the McDowell Mountains, which rise to a little over 4,000 feet directly behind and provide a dramatic, amphitheatral backdrop. The hillside had been used by the prehistoric Hohokam for hunting and other ceremonial and ritual purposes, and the traces they left in the form of petroglyphs and artifacts added to the site's special atmosphere. Wright laid out the buildings along a lateral spine paralleling the northwest trending range of mountains, using 45-degree diagonal shifts to establish axial alignments with surrounding landmarks and to give the projecting main terrace prow a forceful connection with the desert. The individual buildings themselves were constructed of stone, wood, and canvas as permanent versions of the Ocatilla cabins. The angled stone walls, parapets, and substructures were created by a process of agglomera-

Wright in the drafting room of Taliesin West, 1951.

tion in which the variously colored volcanic boulders found in abundance at the site were placed in forms that were filled with a concrete mix and then removed after the stones had been consolidated. Heavy redwood frames were clamped over the tops of the low walls to carry panels of luminous canvas that could either slide back and forth or flip in or out to provide ventilation.

The interior spaces vary from ones almost cave-like in feel, such as Wright's office at the entrance or the so-called kiva at the intersection of the pergola and loggia, to those intentionally tent-like in character, such as the drafting room and main living space, called the garden room. But it is not really the enclosed spaces that define the architecture and experience of Taliesin West. What is much more significant are the spaces between and around the buildings—the walkways, bridges, platforms, and terraces that not only connect building to building but link the entire complex to the mountains and valley surrounding it and to the prehistoric usages associated with them. Axial paths align with key mountain peaks and topographical features to direct the movement of body and eye. Often, as at the small triangular prow opposite Wright's office, or on the stepped pyramidal base above the pool in front of the drafting room, one of the numerous Hohokam petroglyph boulders found nearby has been positioned to mark a point of orientation and thus endow the connection to the landscape with a meaningful temporal resonance.

The first visitors to write about Taliesin West were all struck by the "extraordinary" and "magical" quality of the place. Many resorted to ancient, prehistoric, or primitive parallels, such as were common in the contemporary discourse of Abstract Expressionism, to account for their perceptions. Henry-Russell Hitchcock spoke in 1942 of "the almost prehistoric grandeur" of the complex. Philip Johnson was astounded by the orchestration of movement through the site, which he described as involving notions of the "hieratic" and the "processional." Fowler McCormick, a friend of the Wrights who wintered nearby in Scottsdale, told Wright that he felt there was something "primitive" in what had been achieved. Elizabeth Gordon, editor of *House Beautiful*, wondered why "the massive walls look as if they had been cast in place 100,000 years ago," noting that when they were completed "the effect must have been that of a magnificent ruin." Others, like George Nelson, while remarking on the "barbaric" and "savage" character of the architecture's forms, explained them more empirically as a sympathetic response to the physical appearance of the landscape. Almost more important to him was the "overwhelming…feeling of luxury" Taliesin West projected, the expression of a concept of total design that revealed itself most fully in the enclosure of space "as if it were precious."[5]

The photographs Ezra Stoller took on his first trip to Wright's winter headquarters reflect Nelson's more than any other point of view. While many of the images give a wonderful sense of the overall form of the different buildings and how the materials used in construction were exploited to evoke a strong desert presence, Stoller seems best and most at home, as it were, in capturing a sense of the sheltering quality of the structures and, especially, the way in which interior courtyards and rooms provide serene and tranquil oases from the desert's harshness. This is as true of the magnificent view of the interior of the drafting room as it is of the Wright living quarters and the garden room. Seen from the far end, with a golden harp in the foreground, or looking toward the atrium-like "museum garden" in the opposite direction, Stoller's views of the canvas-covered living space of the Fellowship are, as one of the captions in the *Fortune* piece notes, "suggestive of the great silken tents of Oriental potentates."[6] Unlike Pedro Guerrero's slightly earlier photographs where some of the buildings are under construction and others are seen in relation to key features of the surrounding landscape, Stoller's images emphasize neither the hard work that building and maintaining a professional way of life in the desert entailed nor the more mythic and ritualistic meanings given to it by the mapping of the prehistoric horizon of the site onto the present. Stoller makes Taliesin West, as the *Fortune* article reminds us, "the most luxurious sight imaginable in a land of rocks and cactus."[7]

Stoller was concerned with the fact that he seemed unable to capture in any single shot either a sense of "the sequencing of spaces at Taliesin West" or the overall relationship of the complex to its site. "I kept trying to get more by moving the camera farther back," he said, "but that effort was futile. Best was to suggest the whole through details."[8] He got a chance to try again when he was asked in 1950 by Wright himself, who had come to admire Stoller's work, to do a more "complete" series of photographs, some of which were eventually published in a spread in *Look* magazine, including the new light tower, cabaret-theater, and renovated Sun Cottage.[9] His photographs of January 1951 give more scope both to the relationship between buildings and landscape and to the organization of space between buildings. The views of the entrance area now show how the path of movement is manipulated and controlled by changes in level and direction. The head-on perspective down the length of the pergola brings into focus the standing stone framed by the bridge in the distance and relates it to the Hohokam petroglyph boulder in the foreground as well as to the mountains beyond. The views from the south-facing terrace prow now seem less about the structure of the buildings and more about their relation to the sky and mountains. The prehistoric boulder within the angle of the drafting room and dining room takes on the significance it was intended to have, just as the close-up views of the far end of the pergola now reveal the importance the various traces of prehistoric occupation play in the orientation of sight and movement.

Comparing the results of Stoller's two campaigns reveals more than a change in the photographer's vision. The pictures also show how much Wright had altered Taliesin West, and thus give one more clue as to how its architecture can be understood in the larger context of modernist thought. Wright never stopped adding to the complex or changing what he had already done. This, of course, was also true at Taliesin. But at Taliesin West the context was much grander and the vision more fittingly expansive. Ultimately, Wright intended to extend the axes and sight lines all the way to Black Mountain in the east and Thompson Peak in the north by means of long rows of standing stones. The desire was for total control of the visual environment through design. This modernist dream has been shared by many artists and architects. One thinks of Eliel Saarinen at Cranbrook or Mies at IIT or, more recently, Donald Judd in Marfa, Texas. Both Wright's Taliesin West and Judd's Marfa, despite the fact that the latter is mainly retrofitted, show the extreme to which the modernist concept of total design could be taken by an artist unwilling to be confronted with anything that he has not submitted to his own visual order.

But Wright, the more radical of the two, went so far as to customize the automobile that annually conveyed him from Wisconsin to Arizona and back so that, even between his two domains, he could control the visual environment around him. A semicircular opera window in his "Cherokee red" Lincoln Continental Cabriolet framed the passing scene in a perspicuously Wrightian geometric form. We can see this car in the background of Stoller's photograph of the light tower at Taliesin West, just beneath the red metal basin of the circular fountain. Stoller's forced perspective, intentionally or not, fully comprehends the pervasive character of Wright's vision and at the same time stamps that vision with its own telling form.

1. George Nelson's "Wright's Houses" was published in *Fortune*, August 1946, 116–25. No previous publication had compared the two complexes. Two of Stoller's photographs of the Wright living quarters at Taliesin West appeared concurrently in Winthrop Sergeant, "Frank Lloyd Wright," *Life*, 12 August 1946, 84.

2. This is explained by Wright in an announcement sent out on the opening of the studio added to his Oak Park House in 1898. It is reproduced in *John Lloyd Wright, My Father Who Is on Earth* (1946; rev. ed., Carbondale and Edwardsville: Southern Illinois University Press, 1994), 22.

3. Richard W. Bock, *Memoirs of an American Artist*, ed. Dorathi Bock Pierre (Los Angeles: C. C. Publishing Co., 1989), 138.

4. For an extended discussion and analysis of Taliesin West, see my book *The Architecture of Frank Lloyd Wright* (Princeton: Princeton University Press, 1996), 254–97.

5. Henry-Russell Hitchcock, *In the Nature of Materials: The Buildings of Frank Lloyd Wright, 1887–1941* (New York: Duell, Sloan and Pearce, 1942), 97; Philip Johnson, "100 Years, Frank Lloyd Wright and Us," *Pacific Architect and Builder* (March 1957): 13, 35–6; repr. in Johnson, *Writings* (New York: Oxford University Press, 1979), 196–8; Bruce Brooks Pfeiffer,

ed., *Frank Lloyd Wright: Letters to Apprentices* (Fresno: Press at California State University, 1982), 31; Elizabeth Gordon, "One Man's House," *House Beautiful*, December 1946, 195; and Nelson, "Wright's Houses," 116.

6. Nelson, "Wright's Houses," 123.

7. Ibid.

8. William S. Saunders, *Modern Architecture: Photographs by Ezra Stoller* (New York: Abrams, 1990), 74.

9. Wright to Stoller, 1 March 1950, Frank Lloyd Wright Archives, The Frank Lloyd Wright Foundation, Taliesin West, Scottsdale, AZ. Stoller had planned to make the trip in April 1950 but could not get there before the Fellowship was to leave for Wisconsin. He finally made it in the second week of January 1951. Wright was extremely disappointed in the *Look* article. He wrote to Stoller: "I didn't think the views you contributed to the *Look* coverage were your best work at Taliesin West" (25 January 1952, Frank Lloyd Wright Archives). Stoller responded by blaming it on the "low quality of the reproductions," saying "I couldn't even recognize the pictures as my work—or even yours for that matter." Stoller to Wright, 7 February 1952, Frank Lloyd Wright Archives. See "Journey to Taliesin West," *Look* 16 (1 January 1952): 28–31.

Plates

Drawings & Plans

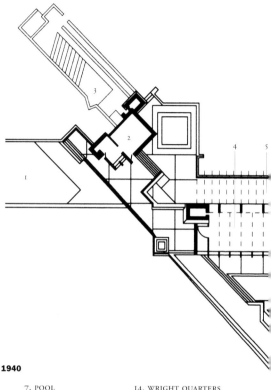

Taliesin West, plan in 1940

1. ENTRANCE COURT
2. WRIGHT OFFICE
3. CABARET THEATER
   (1950 ADDITION)
4. DRAFTING ROOM
5. PERGOLA
6. DINING ROOM

7. POOL
8. SUNK DESERT GARDEN
9. TERRACE PROW
10. TERRACE
11. LOGGIA
12. KIVA
13. GARDEN ROOM

14. WRIGHT QUARTERS
15. GARDEN
16. LANAE
17. POOL
18. BADMINTON COURTS
19. APPRENTICE COURT
20. PATH TO SUN COTTAGE

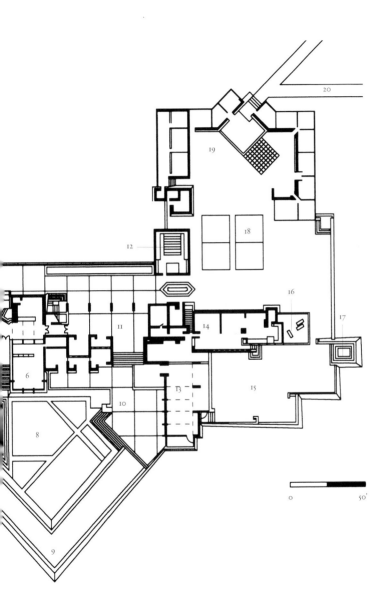

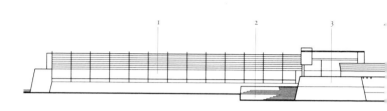

Taliesin West, south elevation/section

1. DRAFTING ROOM   4. APARTMENTS   10. WRIGHT LIVING

2. TERRACE STEPS   5. LOGGIA   QUARTERS

3. DINING ROOM   6. GARDEN ROOM

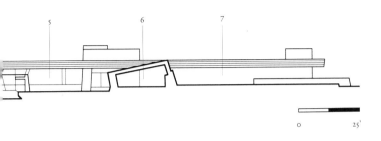

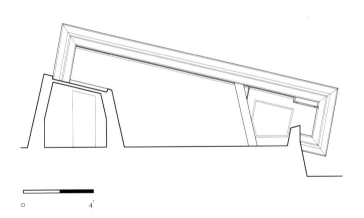

Taliesin West, section through work room

Key to Photographs

[*] *All photographs taken by Ezra Stoller in 1963.*

Published by
Princeton Architectural Press
37 East Seventh Street
New York, NY 10003

For a catalog of books published by Princeton Architectural Press, call toll free 800.722.6657
or visit www.papress.com

Editor & book design: Mark Lamster
Jacket design: Sara E. Stemen
Drawings & Plans by Dan Herman & Linda Chung
Drawings & Plans appear courtesy of the Frank Lloyd Wright Foundation, Scottsdale, AZ

Acknowledgments: I would like to thank my colleagues at Esto Photographics, especially
Kent Draper and Laura Bolli; Mary Doyle and Mike Kimines of TSI for their help in
preparing these images; Oskar Munoz of the Frank Lloyd Wright Archives for his assistance
in providing documentary materials for the drawings and plans; and Mark Lamster for his
support from start to finish—Erica Stoller

Princeton Architectural Press acknowledges Ann Alter, Eugenia Bell, Jan Cigliano, Jane
Garvie, Caroline Green, Beth Harrison, Clare Jacobson, Mirjana Javornik, Therese Kelly,
Leslie Ann Kent, Sara Moss, Anne Nitschke, Lottchen Shivers, and Jennifer Thompson of
Princeton Architectural Press—Kevin C. Lippert, publisher

For the licensing of Ezra Stoller images, contact Esto Photographics.
Fine art reproductions of Stoller prints are available through the James Danziger Gallery.

Printed in Hong Kong

Library of Congress Cataloging-in-Publication Data
Frank Lloyd Wright's Taliesin West / photographs by Ezra Stoller ;
   introduction by Neil Levine.
      p.   cm. -- (Building blocks)
   Includes bibliographical references.
   ISBN 1-56898-202-X (cloth : alk. paper)
   1. Wright, Frank Lloyd (1967–1959)--Homes and haunts--Arizona--
Scottsdale Pictorial works. 2. Taliesin West (Ariz.) Pictorial works.
3. Scottsdale (Ariz.)--Buildings, structures, etc.   I. Stoller, Ezra.
II. Title: Taliesin West. III. Series: Building blocks series (New York, N.Y.)
NA737.W7A4   1999B
779'.47468--DC21   98-52455
                                                          CIP